AF575284

GRANDMOTHERS
have already
earned their wings

San Diego, California
U.S.A.

Selected text by Amy Spitler

ISBN 0-7416-1302-6

www.havocpub.com

Made in Korea

For my dearest
Grandmother,
with love always,

REAP WHAT IS SOWN
PEACE
JOY
HOPE
LOVE
Patience
Justice
Loyalty
Prayers
Honesty
FAITH
TRUST
HUGS
Integrity
Reverence
Gratitude
Compassion

Some lessons in life
are difficult,
while others show our gift,
but all are valuable tools
for understanding
all that makes our life rich.

REAP WHAT IS SOWN

HOPE

REAP WHAT IS SOWN

Your stories told
of bygone times,
make bright the
dimness of the past
and help me see
with vivid colors,
how my own dreams
will come to pass.

A grandmother
holds your hand
when you are scared.
She makes cold evenings warm.
For it is the magical stories
she tells you at night,
that carry you
through the storms.

You may count
your blessings
by all the little
angels in your life.

Like a pebble
tossed into a lake,
creating ripples so far
from the center,
so is the impression
a grandmother makes
in the lives of the people
who love her.

Her wisdom is like
a stream that flows,
in which the stones of life
are clearly seen,
yet gently polishes
each jagged edge,
until what was once rough
shines with a brilliant sheen.

Reflected in
each other's eyes
are both the future
and the past.
A grandmother
and grandchild
see a connection
that will last.

Between
grandmother
and grandchild
is an openness of spirit
and a love that is
living history.

When sharing her story,
it is a grandmother's goal
to paint a picture
for her loved ones,
that is both
charming and whole.

A family that shares
is a family that cares

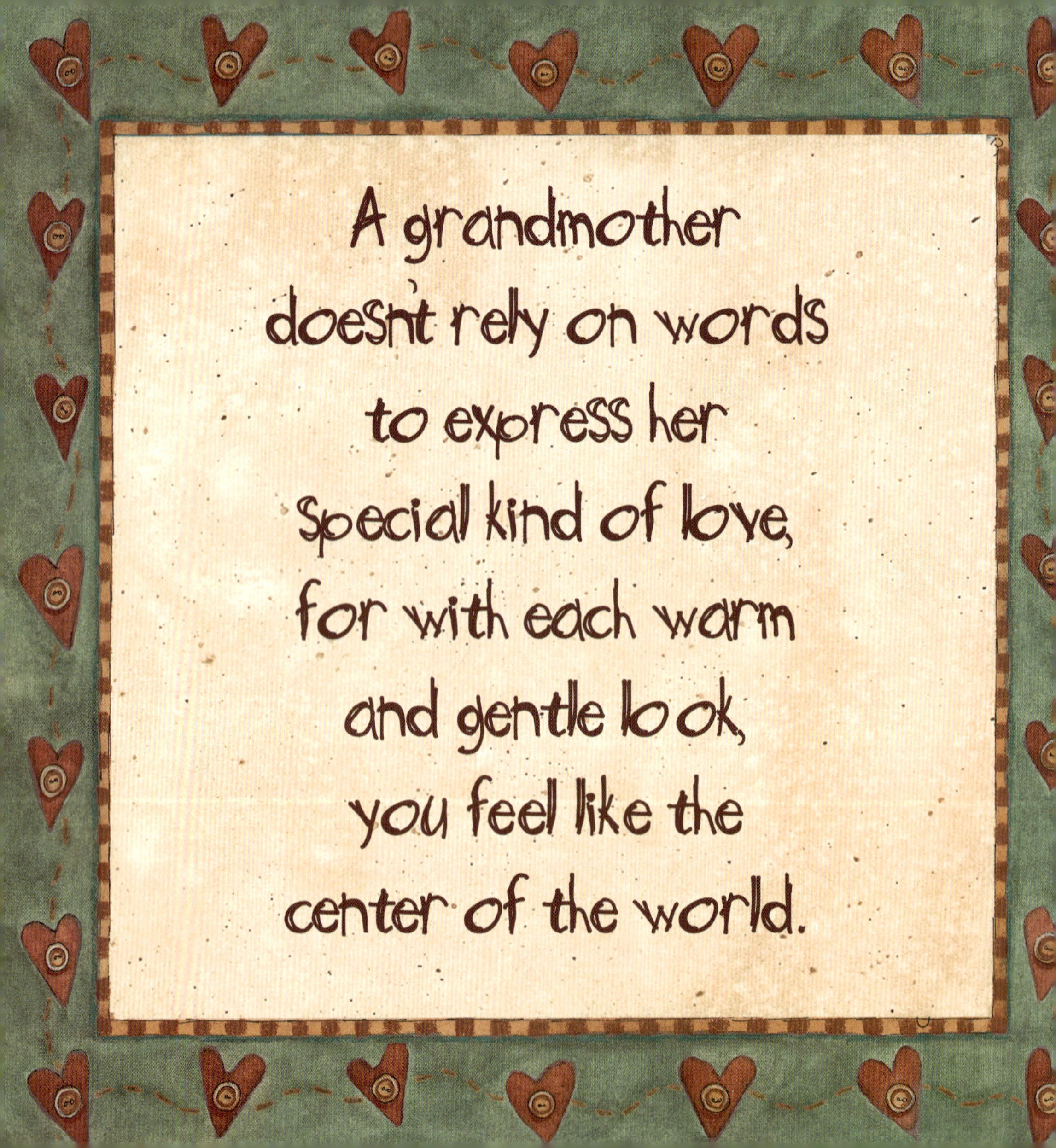
A grandmother
doesn't rely on words
to express her
special kind of love,
for with each warm
and gentle look,
you feel like the
center of the world.

Grandmothers
teach with tenderness
that kindness heals the heart,
and that it's better
to reach out to others
than to set
yourself apart.

Grandmothers
make childhood
special because
they truly understand
the magical nature
of youth.

Grandmothers
know that
simple pleasures,
when shared,
can make your life
rich beyond compare.

Good fortune
is a life
blessed with a
grandmother.

Like a patchwork
of brilliant colors,
hand-stitched with
love so strong,
a grandmother binds
together generations
and reveals a pattern
of life to which you belong.

THIMBLE THIMBLE WHO'S GOT THE THIMBLE?
THE LESSONS LEARNED IN MOTHERHOOD ARE PERFECTED AS A GRANDMOTHER

A grandmother
is special in very many ways.
She is bright
and a cheerful friend,
shining with more glory
than the sun's rays.

Holding her hand,
sharing a warm
embrace,
are special moments
spent with Grandmother
which can never
be replaced.

REAP WHAT IS SOWN
PEACE
JOY
HOPE
LOVE
She can open
your eyes to
nature's beauty,
sharing her own
secret glee,
REAP WHAT IS SOWN
REAP WHAT IS SOWN
REAP WHAT IS SOWN

REAP WHAT IS SOWN
PEACE
JOY
REAP WHAT IS SOWN
REAP WHAT IS SOWN
at the miracle of
a flower's bloom,
a bird's song,
or the majesty
of a tree.
HOPE
LOVE
REAP WHAT IS SOWN

GRANDMOTHERS
REMIND US THAT WE ARE BLESSED

Like the promise
of a rainbow after
a gentle morning rain,
a grandmother has
the power to brighten
even the darkest day.

She engages you
with her imagination
and creates a palette
of colors with her words,
painting the present
with a richness of wonder,
a grandmother's
gift to the world.

She can tell
if you are sad,
never needing to know
the reason why.
Grandmother is the
greatest comforter,
finding the silver lining
in every sigh.

A grandmother's riches,
no matter how young
or how old,
are measured in her
grandchildren's kisses,
to her,
they are more precious
than gold.

A simple, yet great, pleasure in life

is giving a kiss to a sleeping child

While all gems
are precious,
some have a unique shine.
And in the setting
of a lovely family,
a grandmother's
sparkle is the
most divine.

It is because
her heart is open
to all of life's possibilities
that grandmother
truly inspires us
to become the person
we wish to be.

GRANDMOTHERS
LOVE TO SPOIL
My
Country Home

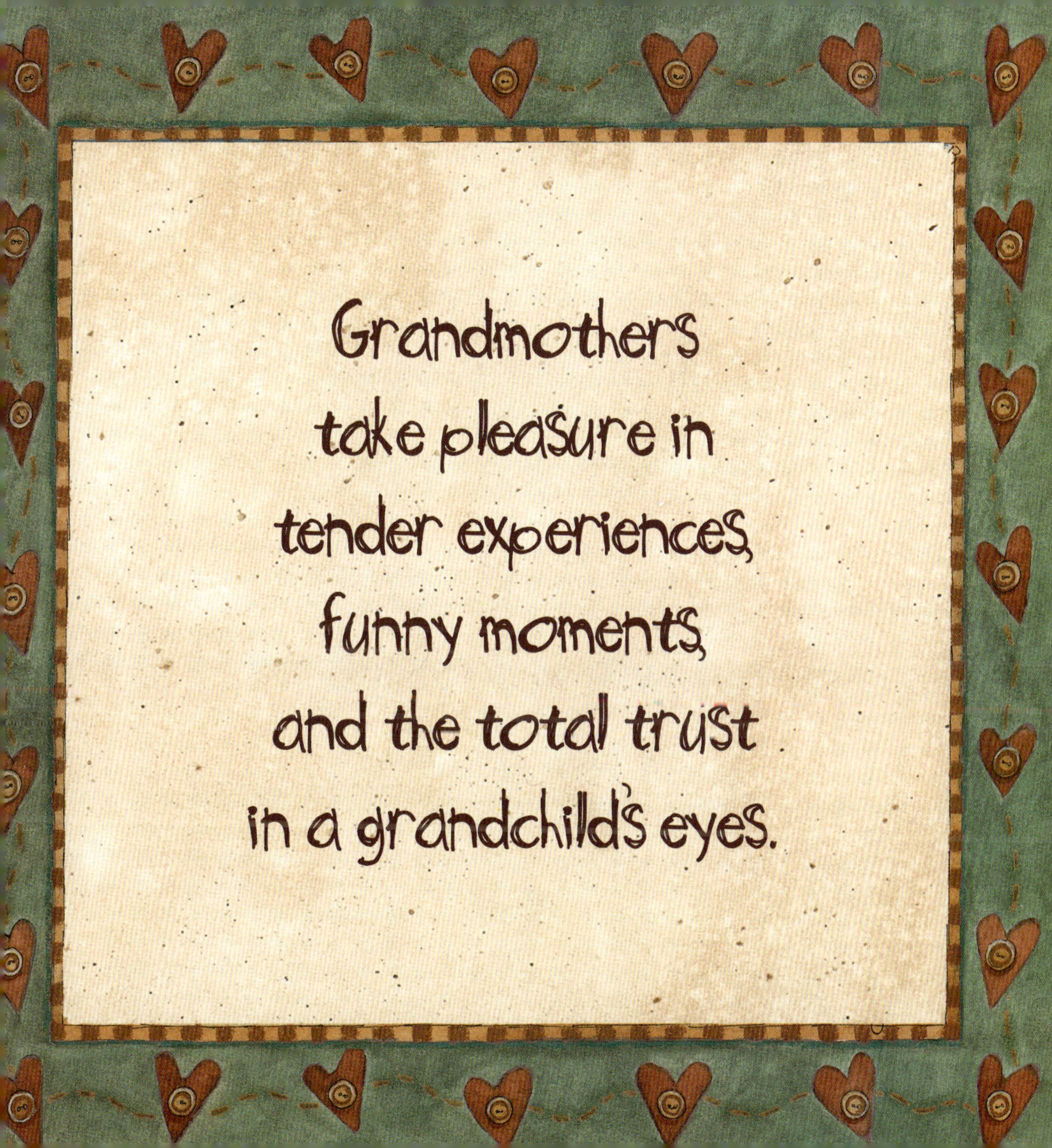
Grandmothers
take pleasure in
tender experiences,
funny moments,
and the total trust
in a grandchild's eyes.

A grandmother
has the soul
of a little girl
with a lifetime
of experiences.

Grandmothers dote,
and give lots of kisses,
but their favorite
thing of all is to
grant children's wishes.

All my life,
my grandmother
has helped to build
my character.
Her love has
shown me the way
to become the person
I am today.

My grandmother
is an endless source
of hope and inspiration,
and that is why
she'll always
have my love
and admiration.

Garden Journal

A grandmother
gives of her heart
with no conditions
in mind.
She is selfless in her love,
a presence so
warm and kind.

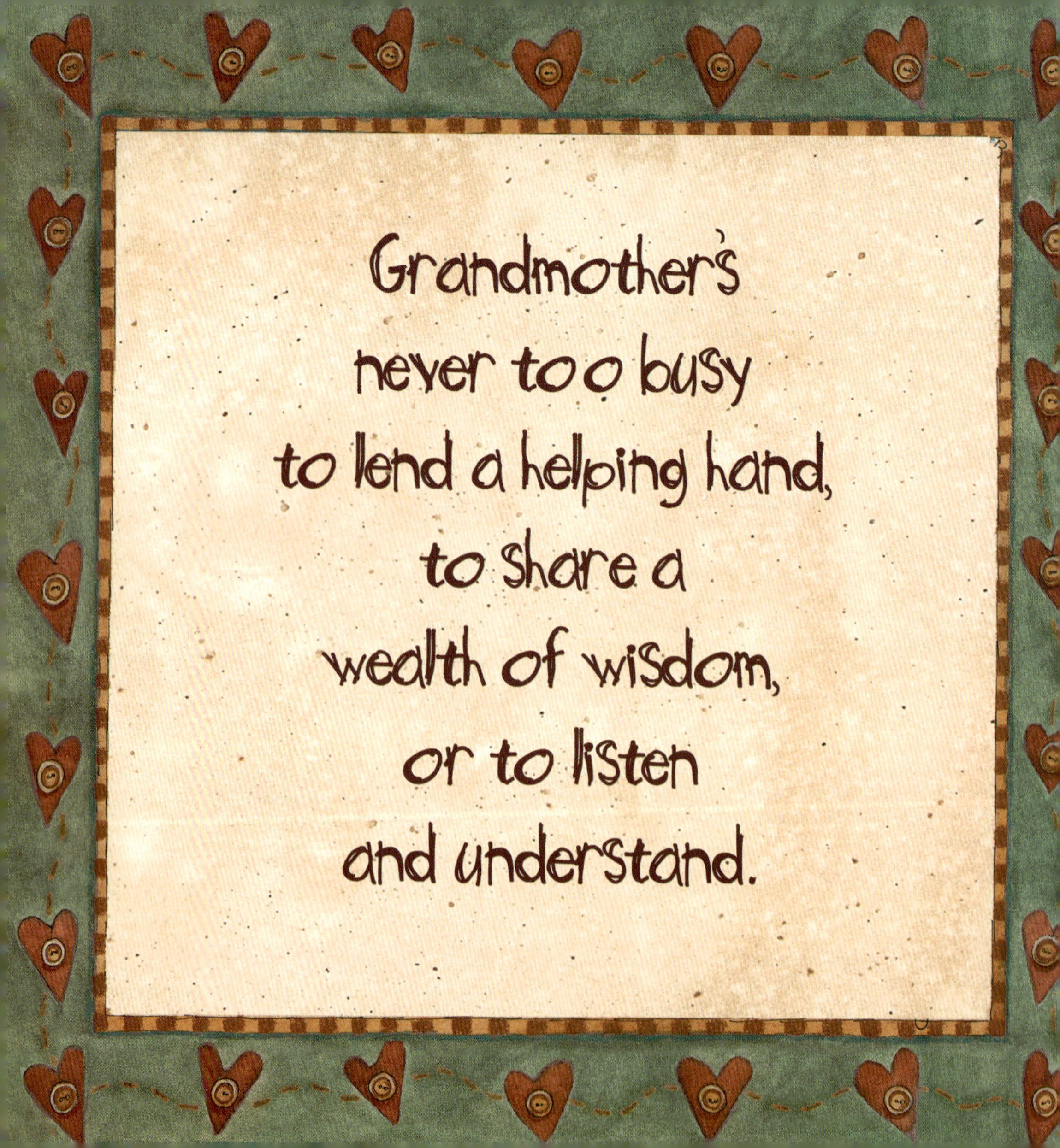
Grandmother's
never too busy
to lend a helping hand,
to share a
wealth of wisdom,
or to listen
and understand.

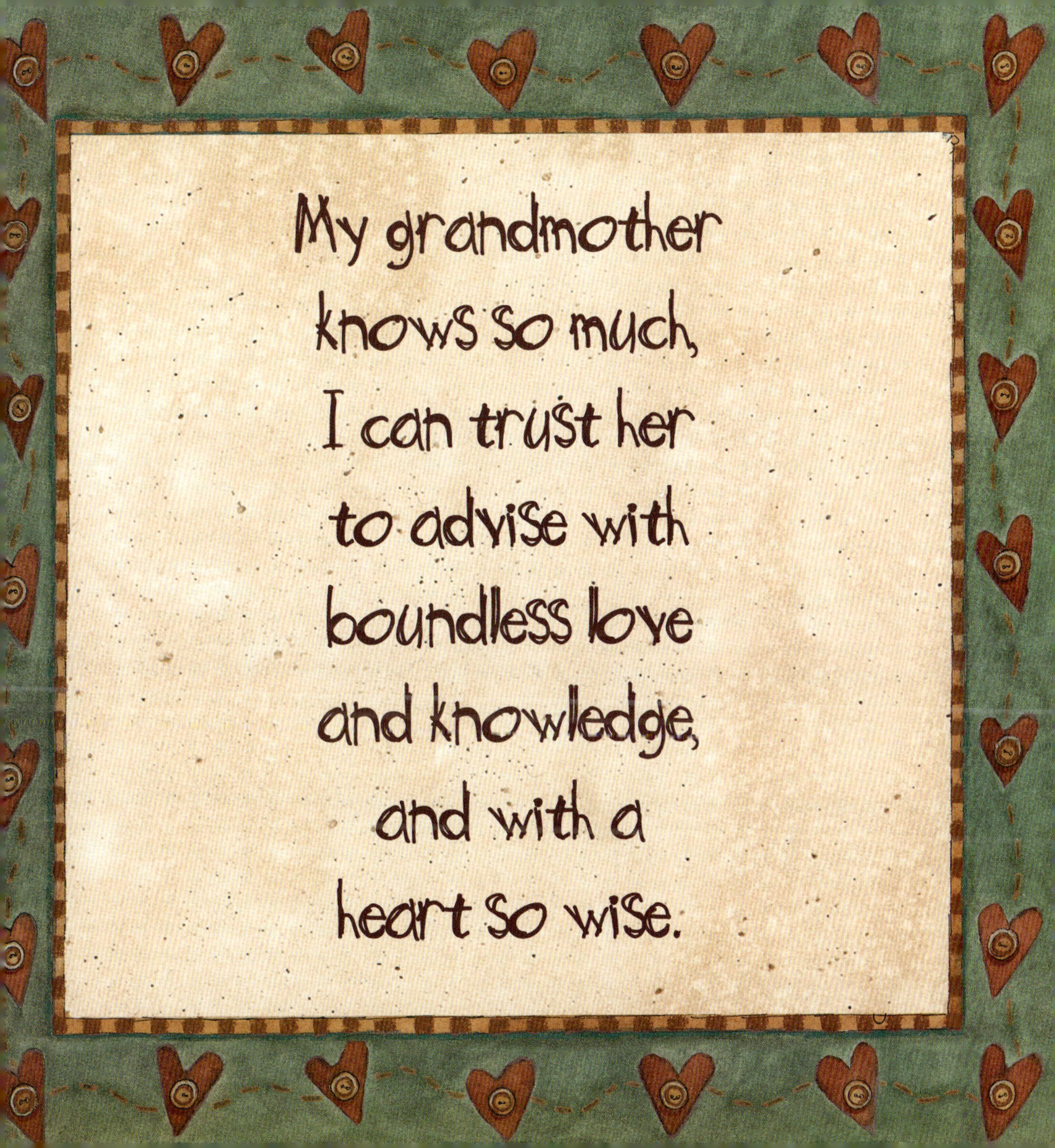
My grandmother
knows so much,
I can trust her
to advise with
boundless love
and knowledge,
and with a
heart so wise.

Your encouragement
helped me grow.
Your pride was food
for my soul,
and by voicing so loudly
your love for me,
I feel contented
and whole.

You have the
softness of a petal,
with roots the
strength of steel,
and thorns to
fend off trouble,
with a sweetness
true and real.

Grandmothers
are angels
with
invisible wings.

Becoming a
grandmother is a
blessing from above,
for within
your heart,
you find a new
kind of love.

PEACE

REAP WHAT IS SOWN

JOY

Grandmothers
share the knowledge
that being
who you are
is truly a blessing.

REAP WHAT IS SOWN

LOVE

You are always
there for me,
whether things are
right or wrong,
and I am blessed to have you
as my grandmother,
and will treasure you
my whole life long.